16 $\frac{4}{11}$ : $\frac{10}{11}$

# YOUR PET
# IGUANA

## REVISED EDITION

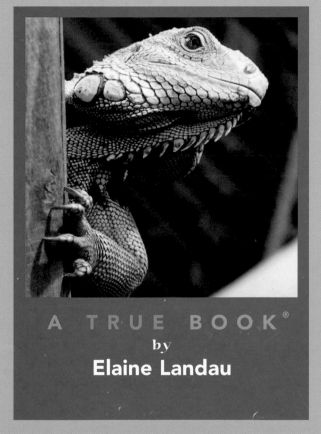

### A TRUE BOOK®

by
**Elaine Landau**

*Children's Press*®
A Division of Scholastic Inc.

New York  Toronto  London  Auckland  Sydney
Mexico City  New Delhi  Hong Kong
Danbury, Connecticut

A baby green iguana

Content Consultant
**Robin Downing, DVM, CVA, DAAPM**
*Hospital Director, Windsor Veterinary Clinic
Windsor, Colorado*

*Reading Consultant*
**Cecilia Minden-Cupp, PhD**
*Former Director, Language and Literacy Program
Harvard Graduate School of Education*

*Author's Dedication*
**For Dr. Barbara Muina—a wonderful doctor and human being**

*The photograph on the cover shows a green iguana on its owner's shoulder. The photograph on the title page shows a green iguana at a zoo.*

Library of Congress Cataloging-in-Publication Data
Landau, Elaine.
    Your pet iguana / by Elaine Landau.—Rev. ed.
        p. cm. — (A true book)
    Includes index.
    ISBN-10: 0-531-16790-9 (lib. bdg.)        0-531-15468-8 (pbk.)
    ISBN-13: 978-0-531-16790-8 (lib. bdg.)    978-0-531-15468-7 (pbk.)
    1. Green iguanas as pets—Juvenile literature. I. Title. II. Series.
SF459.I38L35 2006
639.3'95—dc22

                                                                    2006004421

# Contents

The green iguana has a row of spines along its back.

# An Iguana and You

Would you like a pet that looks like a small dinosaur? Would you like a pet that is covered with scales and has a row of **spines** along its back? Would you like a green iguana as a pet? Before you say yes, there are many things to think about.

Many people like green iguanas. A pet iguana is not for everyone, however. When a green iguana grows up, it can be as long as 6 feet (1.8 meters). That's about the length of an adult man lying down!

Keeping an iguana can cost a lot of money. It is also a lot of work. Getting a pet iguana is a decision kids must make with a parent. You will need an adult to help you care for this pet.

A small green iguana will grow quickly—and live for as many as fifteen years.

An iguana can live for more than fifteen years. That means you will be responsible for your pet for a long time. So before you say, "I wanna iguana," read on.

It is best to start with a baby green iguana.

# Picking an Iguana

Some people dream of buying a full-grown iguana. They feel it is the closest they will ever come to owning a dinosaur. However, it is better to start with a baby iguana.

An older iguana from the wild won't get used to living

in a cage as quickly as a baby iguana. An older, wild iguana will not want to be handled. You should also know that when an older iguana is frightened, it will defend itself with its claws and tail.

There are other things to look for in an iguana. Try to find a young iguana that has been handled by humans. An iguana that is used to people is less likely to panic when you pick it up.

# An Iguana Is No Dog

A pet iguana resting on its owner

**D**o not expect your iguana to act like a dog. It will not greet you after school with warm, wet kisses. Some iguanas never become truly tame, while others might rest comfortably on your shoulder. Iguanas are **cold-blooded** animals. They rely on their surroundings to control their body temperature. Because your body is warm, you are more like a heating pad than a pal to these **lizards**!

An iguana's color can tell you a lot about the animal's health. Baby iguanas should be bright green. A baby iguana that is dark olive green or yellowish may be very ill. Older iguanas should be grayish green. Iguanas can carry serious diseases, so it is important to get a healthy one.

Healthy young iguanas have clear, bright eyes. Also, try to choose an active, alert

Healthy young pet iguanas are bright green.

lizard. The baby iguana you take home should look interested in what's going on around it.

# Lizard Life

**I**guanas are lizards, or **reptiles** with long, scaly bodies, a long tail, and legs. A reptile is a cold-blooded animal that moves on small, short legs or on its belly.

Here are some fascinating facts about iguanas and other lizards:

A marine iguana swimming in the Galápagos Islands

* There are about three thousand **species**, or types, of lizards.
* The marine iguana of the Galápagos Islands is an excellent swimmer and feeds on seaweed.

* When it is in danger, the Texas horned lizard squirts blood from its eyes. It can hit an enemy 10 feet (3 m) away!

A Texas horned lizard

* People usually have green iguanas as pets. Blue iguanas live on the Cayman Islands.

* Lizards have scaly skin made of the same material as human fingernails.

* The tails of some lizards make up about two-thirds of their body length.

# Your Iguana's Home

A baby iguana is about 8 inches (20 centimeters) long. It will be five times that size, and still growing, two years later. So your iguana needs a large cage. An adult iguana needs a cage as long as 8 feet (2 m).

Iguanas need a cage large enough to move around in comfortably.

Don't forget to wash your hands after handling or cleaning up after an iguana.

Big or small, an iguana cage must be cleaned out every day. Always wash your hands after cleaning the cage or handling your iguana.

Be sure to put some sturdy branches in your iguana's cage. Iguanas are excellent climbers. They will climb up on these branches to rest.

An iguana climbs on a branch in its cage.

Iguanas are **tropical** animals. That means they come from the hot, rainy areas of the world called the tropics.

Iguanas need a warm place to live, as well as sunlight. If you live where it is cooler, you can attach special lamps to the cage. Ask at the pet store about other ways to heat and light an iguana cage.

Some owners set aside entire rooms in their homes for their full-grown iguanas.

A green iguana soaks up sunlight under a glass roof.

Iguanas are great swimmers. Some iguana rooms even have small, built-in pools! An iguana doesn't need a fancy home as long as the animal gets enough space and exercise.

If your iguana is in a cage, you should take it out each day. Before you do, close all the windows and doors in the room. Learn which house-plants are poisonous to lizards and put them out of

Iguanas like to climb around the house.

your iguana's reach. Keep other pets, such as dogs or cats, away from the iguana.

Some iguana owners who live in warm areas take their iguanas outdoors to exercise. Tame iguanas wear a special leash.

You can take a pet iguana for a walk on its special leash.

An iguana owner and her pet sit in the Florida sun.

Some iguana owners let their leashed pets climb trees. Others just enjoy sunbathing with their pets!

A pet iguana needs fresh vegetables and fruit.

# Mealtime at the Iguana Cage

Many pet owners feed their animals food from a can, but that's not possible with an iguana. You will have to buy or gather fresh vegetables and fruits for your special pet. It's no small job.

Adult iguanas feed mostly on plants. They eat the leaves and flowers of dandelions and a spiny herb called sow thistle. They also eat clover, alfalfa, bean sprouts, turnip greens, and mulberry leaves.

Iguanas feed on various plants.

Eating too much lettuce isn't healthy for a pet iguana.

You can feed an iguana grated or chopped carrots, sweet potatoes, cabbage, pumpkins, cucumbers, okra, and potatoes. Many iguanas love lettuce, but they should eat only small amounts because it lacks nutrition.

Iguanas also need small amounts of fruits. Apples, pears, strawberries, bananas, peaches, plums, cherries, and blackberries are healthy options. You should peel and finely chop all fruits before feeding them to your iguana.

An iguana's food must be fresh. Spoiled food can make an iguana ill. You should sprinkle vitamins and supplements on your iguana's food twice a week.

Bananas in small pieces are a favorite food for green iguanas.

An outdoor pet iguana has separate bowls for food and water.

A pet iguana must be fed every day. It is a good idea to

feed your iguana at the same time each day. Many owners feed their iguana in the morning to give it time to digest its food before nighttime.

An iguana needs separate food and water bowls. They should be as large as the animal because iguanas like to step in their food and water before eating and drinking! Iguanas also bathe in their water bowls, so the water must be changed daily.

Gentle handling from humans will protect an iguana's long tail from damage.

# Keeping Your Iguana Healthy

Many iguanas become ill and even die because they haven't gotten proper care. Perhaps the most common iguana injury is losing the tail. Rough handling from humans can break off the tail.

Pick up an iguana holding it under the stomach and front legs.

Learn how to handle an iguana. Never grab or carry it by the tail. Hold the iguana under its stomach and front legs and lift gently.

An iguana can lose its tail on purpose. Iguanas in the wild may do this to escape from an enemy that has grasped its tail.

When an iguana's tail breaks off, it is left with a bloody stump. The wound heals by itself in time. Keep the area clean to prevent infection. Your pet's tail should start to grow back in a few months.

An iguana can develop breathing problems in colder

areas. Its nose may be runny. It may lose its appetite. Its color may turn dull gray or yellow. An iguana in this condition must see a **veterinarian**, a doctor who treats animals, immediately.

Regular visits to a veterinarian are an important part of keeping your pet healthy. You need to find a veterinarian who is experienced in treating large lizards or other unusual, or **exotic**, pets.

A veterinarian examines a pet iguana.

Giving your iguana proper care will pay off. If your iguana is healthy, you will enjoy it for many years.

Pet iguanas cannot survive
on their own.

# A Serious Decision

Keeping a green iguana as a pet can be more work than people realize. Sadly, each year, many owners set their unwanted iguanas loose. These animals cannot survive in cool weather or big cities.

Most zoos and animal shelters are unprepared to care for iguanas. Iguana rescue groups work hard to find new owners for abandoned pets. But there aren't nearly enough interested people to meet the need.

Many owners take good care of their pet iguanas. They enjoy the responsibilities and love the company of their quiet, unusual pet. If you and your family are willing and able

An owner plays with her one-year-old pet iguana.

to care for a large tropical lizard, an iguana may be the pet for you.

# To Find Out More

Here are some additional resources to help you learn more about iguanas:

 **Books**

Donovan, Sandra. **Iguana**. Raintree Steck-Vaughn, 2002.

Giles, Bridget. **Iguanas**. Grolier Educational, 2001.

Jango-Cohn, Judith. **Desert Iguanas**. Lerner Publications, 2001.

Lockwood, Sophie. **Iguanas**. Child's World, 2006.

Newman, Chris. **Iguana**. Barron's Educational Series, 2000.

Simon, Elizabeth. **Caring for Your Iguana**. Weigl Publishers, 2005.

Williams, Sarah. **101 Facts About Iguanas**. Gareth Stevens, 2001.

## Organizations and Online Sites

**The Green Iguana Society**
*http://www.greenigsociety.org/*

Check out this site for a glossary of iguana terms, quick tips for new owners, and a "Kids Club" section with a green iguana quiz, an iguana word puzzle, and details about owning an iguana.

**International Iguana Foundation**
1989 Colonial Parkway
Fort Worth, TX 76110
817–759–7177
*http://www.iguanafoundation.org/index.php*

This organization supports conservation of wild iguanas and their habitats. Check out the site to learn more about wild iguanas around the world.

**National Iguana Awareness Day**
*http://www.niad.org/*

Learn more about the responsibilities of owning and caring for an iguana at this site.

45

# Important Words

*cold-blooded* having a body temperature that changes with the temperature of the surroundings

*exotic* unusual or fascinating

*lizards* reptiles (see below) with long, scaly bodies, a long tail, and legs

*reptiles* cold-blooded animals that move on small, short legs—such as alligators, turtles, or lizards—or on their bellies, such as snakes

*species* types of animals that have similar characteristics and a common name

*spines* hard, pointed growths on an animal

*tropical* having to do with the hot, rainy area of the world called the tropics

*veterinarian* a doctor who treats animals

# Index

# Meet the Author

Award-winning author Elaine Landau worked as a newspaper reporter, an editor, and a youth-services librarian before becoming a full-time writer. She has written more than 250 nonfiction books for young people, including True Books on dinosaurs, animals, countries, and food. Ms. Landau has a bachelor's degree in English and journalism from New York University as well as a master's degree in library and information science. She lives with her husband and son in Miami, Florida.

for

Published by Charlesbridge
85 Main Street
Watertown, MA 02472
(617) 926-0329
www.charlesbridge.com

**Library of Congress Cataloging-in-Publication Data**
Czekaj, Jef.
   A call for a new alphabet / Jef Czekaj.
      p. cm.
   Summary: Tired of being near the end of the alphabet, starting few words, and being
governed by grammar rules, X calls for a vote on a new Alphabet Constitution, then
dreams of how life would be if he became a different letter.
   ISBN 978-1-58089-228-5 (reinforced for library use)
   ISBN 978-1-58089-229-2 (softcover)
[1. Alphabet—Fiction. 2. English language—Grammar—Fiction. 3. Voting—Fiction.
4. Humorous stories.] I. Title.
PZ7.C9987Cal 2011
[E]—dc22                                                    2010007534

Printed in Singapore
(hc) 10 9 8 7 6 5 4 3 2 1
(sc) 10 9 8 7 6 5 4 3 2 1

Line art drawn in ink on Bristol paper and then scanned and colored
   on a MacBook Pro using Adobe Photoshop
Display type and text type set in EyeCheck and Cheltenham
Color separations by Chroma Graphics, Singapore
Printed and bound September 2010 by Imago in Singapore
Production supervision by Brian G. Walker
Designed by Martha MacLeod Sikkema

Z was snoozing. It had been a very, very long couple of days.

zebra

Y was also happy to be back where she belonged.

sky

yacht

yo-yo

Ah, it's great to have everything back to normal. Isn't that right, Z? Z? Z?

And so it was that the alphabet remained as it has been since you and I were young. X proudly took his place third to last in the alphabet.

flying fox

EXIT→

There may not be many words that start with me, but there are plenty that have me in them!

tuxedo

exercising ox

ax

box of wax

saxophone

Needless to say, the alphabet was shocked and reacted in many unique ways.

G gasped.

B breathed a sigh of relief.

O offered his opinions.

F fainted.

J jumped for joy.

R, for some reason, roller-skated away.

A hush fell over the crowd. If X's vote was a "yes," the alphabet that we all learned in school would be thrown out.

My distinguished consonants and vowels. I stand before you to humbly cast my vote.

Yesterday I was **sure** we needed a new alphabet. I was sick of my lowly role and jealous of all the other letters.

X exploded through the chamber doors.

As X charged up the stairs of Alphabet Hall, he heard the voice of Judge J.

X's dream continued. . . .

X was exasperated. As his dream continued, he met more letters.

First he dreamed that he was S. He ran from word to word, finding that most words became plural—meaning more than one of something—with the addition of an S at the end.

Of course, there were exceptions.

Sorry, we don't need you here.

Eventually he drifted off to sleep, where he had the strangest dreams.

That night X was so excited that he could barely sleep.

I wonder what it's like to have the rules and responsibilities of other letters.

The letters cheered.

And so the consonants and vowels retired to their homes . . .

to think about the most important decision of their lives.

The letters were at odds over X's ideas.

Y was yelling at W.

S was sobbing.

R was ranting at T.

The alphabet seemed to be falling apart
when suddenly . . .

X caused quite a commotion. Never before had someone suggested that the alphabet be altered. The confused letters gathered to listen to X's explosive words.

yawn

Helpful H explained.

That's the way it's always been.

The alphabet always starts with A, then comes B, then C, all the way to Z.

See, you're **way** down here.

The alphabet needs order, just like grammar needs rules.

Well, I'm SICK of all these rules!

Every letter, that is, except for X.
X was excited and exasperated.

Every letter was happy and content.

**It was an average day in Alphabet City.**
S was soaking up some sun, bearded B
was bouncing a ball, R was roller-skating,
and there was P in the pool.

# A CALL FOR A NEW ALPHABET

Jef Czekaj

i◠i Charlesbridge

WAVE

P9-CAA-080

SPLAT

for

Published by Charlesbridge
85 Main Street
Watertown, MA 02472
(617) 926-0329
www.charlesbridge.com

**Library of Congress Cataloging-in-Publication Data**
Czekaj, Jef.
   A call for a new alphabet / Jef Czekaj.
      p. cm.
   Summary: Tired of being near the end of the alphabet, starting few words, and being
governed by grammar rules, X calls for a vote on a new Alphabet Constitution, then
dreams of how life would be if he became a different letter.
   ISBN 978-1-58089-228-5 (reinforced for library use)
   ISBN 978-1-58089-229-2 (softcover)
[1. Alphabet—Fiction. 2. English language—Grammar—Fiction. 3. Voting—Fiction.
4. Humorous stories.] I. Title.
PZ7.C9987Cal 2011
[E]—dc22                                                    2010007534

Printed in Singapore
(hc) 10 9 8 7 6 5 4 3 2 1
(sc) 10 9 8 7 6 5 4 3 2 1

Line art drawn in ink on Bristol paper and then scanned and colored
   on a MacBook Pro using Adobe Photoshop
Display type and text type set in EyeCheck and Cheltenham
Color separations by Chroma Graphics, Singapore
Printed and bound September 2010 by Imago in Singapore
Production supervision by Brian G. Walker
Designed by Martha MacLeod Sikkema

Z was snoozing. It had been a very, very long couple of days.

Y was also happy to be back where she belonged.

sky

yacht

yo-yo

Ah, it's great to have everything back to normal. Isn't that right, Z? Z? Z?

And so it was that the alphabet remained as it has been since you and I were young. X proudly took his place third to last in the alphabet.

Needless to say, the alphabet was shocked and reacted in many unique ways.

G gasped.

B breathed a sigh of relief.

whew

O offered his opinions.

blah
blah
blah
blah

F fainted.

J jumped for joy.

R, for some reason, roller-skated away.

ZZip!

As X charged up the stairs of Alphabet Hall, he heard the voice of Judge J.